Marta Martín

You Can Heal Yourself

With

REIKI

Questions & Answers

A book that sheds light on how the Reiki technique
acts upon yourself to restore balance
on a physical, mental and emotional level

Title: You can heal yourself with Reiki: Questions & Answers

ISBN: 978-84-612-7279-2

Editorial supervision by Kay Butler

Cover design by James Alexis Fontaine: fontaine.20@gmail.com

Talig-Shekasten caligraphy created by M.ES. Rouya

1st Edition, November 2008

Editor's note: The writer is a native Spanish whose second language is English. It has been the editor's intention to keep her own natural voice as the copy editing work has been done.

For more information about this book:

info@saraswati.es

healyourselfwithreiki@gmail.com

You are invited to send the author your questions about Reiki
to any of the addresses above.

Should you wish to participate in a Reiki course with the
author, please send an e-mail to:

info@saraswati.es

healyourselfwithreiki@gmail.com

To all students
who made this book possible

Wait till you look within yourself
and see what is there.
O seeker,
One leaf in that Garden
Is worth more than all of Paradise!

— Rumi

From: "A Garden Beyond Paradise — Love Poems of Rumi"
by Jonathan Star

Contents

Introduction 1

First Questions About Reiki 3

The Layers of a Human Being and the Effect of Thoughts ..23

Treatments on Oneself.....................................41

Treatments on Others 53

Distance Reiki 67

Reactions 79

Reiki and Meditation 91

Attunement Experiences 99

This book is the answer to an insight that came up at an "attunement" in a Reiki course. The profound atmosphere of this most relevant session activates in students the ability to convey the *vital energy* known as Reiki.

During this period, apprentices enter a meditative state and tap into their own inner silence; this allows them to perceive "all that is ever present." We take our attention away from mental activity and direct it toward other centers within our system, extraordinary sources of deep love and peace.

Attunement is the name given to an intense transmission of the vital energy called Reiki, which takes place from the teacher to each student. This process opens up a series of channels within the energy system of a human being who from then on is able to channel through his whole body, and especially through the palms of his hands, an enormous current of vital energy. Such a skill, once awakened, will never be lost, and it will continually unfold the more it is practiced and the more the student allows for its development.

Reiki is everywhere. It permeates the ether. We learn to use it and we apply it to ourselves or others in order to restore balance on a physical, mental, and emotional level. It should be understood as a complement to conventional medical treatments; it has been widely used as a relaxation and antistress technique.

This book has been designed for every reader to understand Reiki on a deep level, as you read along the questions and answers. It has been written for those of you who feel curious about this method, as well as for all of you who already use it and wish to deepen your understanding about the way this energy works; it is my intention to offer you a greater clarity to help you refine your Reiki practice and offer top quality treatments.

Many books have been published about Reiki that show exercises and various techniques, and therefore I will not go deeply into that. I will focus on shedding light on what this energy really is, where it comes from, how it works within ourselves and within those who receive our treatments, and especially what we can do to take the most advantage of the process.

We are talking about a technique that uses an energy that is "invisible" to our eyes. Nevertheless, its effects have been widely proven. Reiki is used in many hospitals in the United States, it is available within the Social Security System in the United Kingdom, and it is considered as a Complementary Therapy by the World Health Organization. Eastern philosophies, meditation studies, and many years of extensive practice have been considered in order to offer the reader a larger vision of Reiki´s *modus operandi*, as this knowledge holds the key to deeply understand the effects of Reiki on oneself or others.

At the advanced levels of this learning, the student is invited to start a regular meditation practice. Reiki triggers meditative states and in the same way, when a person is able to hold an inner meditative state, the stream of Reiki flows greatly. When we meditate, we take our attention away from the constant mental activity, and this brings about great peace and balance within ourselves; the vibration of our energy is heightened, it becomes purer, closer to the range vibration of Reiki: a light of love. When we meditate we become the ideal arena for Reiki to flow through us.

Marta Martín

FIRST QUESTIONS

ABOUT REIKI

First Questions About Reiki

This section answers the first questions that usually come up regarding Reiki. It is my intention that, as much as possible, the answers evoke a very clear mental image of the way this method operates. Since we are working with an energy that is not visible, we will also use analogies to help us understand the various concepts of something so ethereal yet so effective.

Everything regarding Reiki may seem a little abstract at first, since it is our tendency to accept only that which our mind can measure—everything within the confines of what it already knows. Nevertheless, the effects of Reiki treatments have been widely proven, although it is a nonvisible energy.

Of all holistic treatments, Reiki is probably the easiest one to learn, since not much information is needed for it to work. Every person is able to channel Reiki. The only essential step is taking a course that *awakens* this skill and you will hold within your hands an endless stream of life that you can convey to yourself or to other people.

Reiki is a restorative method that works on the physical, mental, and emotional levels. It acts upon the origin of any unbalance. It strengthens the immune system, and for this reason it is used in the oncology departments of many hospitals in the United States. It heals scars very quickly, it evokes deep states of inner peace, and so it helps in reducing stress.

What does "Reiki" mean?

Reiki is a Japanese word meaning *vital energy* or *vital force*, and it is also the technique that allows a person to use that energy. Along the Reiki transmission process, the human body acts as a receiver and transmitter of vital force, the hands being the medium through which it is conveyed with a greater potency.

For something like this to be possible, it is essential that a Reiki teacher activates this ability during a course.

Ki already exists within a person and it permeates everything alive. The word *ki* means the same as lifeforce, or *prana,* or *chi.* It is present within the ether and it is the foundation, the support, the essence of everything that exists. Wherever life is, there is Reiki.

What does Reiki look like?

Reiki is light; a bright white light of a golden hue. It is invisible to the eyes because its vibrational frequency is beyond the range of humanly visible frequencies. Yet, it is possible to have a glimpse of Reiki when the practitioner takes on a meditative attitude.

There are two main attributes to Reiki:

- It is pure love

- It is intelligent

The "intelligence" of this vibration can be understood in the same way that we understand Nature as intelligent: Nature "knows" how to maintain and restore balance, and it always finds the means to achieve a perfect equilibrium. As the *vital force* known as Reiki is infused within a person's body, it gradually restores the optimum flow of her own vital energy. As a result, this person enjoys a wonderful feeling of relaxation and wellbeing.

How does Reiki work?

Remember the way you felt when you were a child—the overflowing vitality, so much bliss, waking up in the morning from a restorative sleep full of enthusiasm to start a new day. Although a child also goes through "negative" emotional states, we can observe his or her reactions: He can go totally into anger or some other negative emotion, yet is able to move back into bliss in a matter of seconds, totally forgetting the previous emotion. He responds to whatever is right in front of him in the present moment. He lives in bliss most of his time because his vital energy is flowing freely.

As we grow older, we forget our ability to let go of unwanted emotions, to just jump into the next good feeling, thought, and sensation. We tend to "hook up" to unconstructive emotional states. The circumstance that created our negative response may not exist in our present moment anymore, but we keep talking about it and thinking about it, over and over again, and in this way we perpetuate the feeling that it brought about within us.

Everything that exists is linked to a form of energy and from this perspective we can consider our thoughts and feelings as forms of energy (our neurons communicate through electrical impulses). Does the quality of our thoughts and feelings affect our physical body? Does it affect our energy? Of course! Do we feel the same, physically and emotionally, when we think we are not enough as when we think of and feel our own worth?

Everything that takes place within our energy body (often referred to as the "subtle" body or "astral" body) affects our physical body, and the same happens the other way around. Some theories affirm that physical, mental, or emotional "disease," or illness, is the result of inappropriate nourishment, the continuous repetition of unwanted thoughts and feelings, or a shocking event that triggered a disproportionate emotional discharge through our system.

Also, every thought gives birth to a feeling. Let us consider each negative thought and feeling as a thin energy layer that slightly taints a spot inside us; when we hold such recurring thoughts, a thicker concentration of dense or "negative" energy may be gathered within us, obstructing the free flow of our own vital energy. At whatever place in the body this happens, that area undergoes a depleted vitality. Time goes by and eventually such a blockage, or energy shortage, physically affects whatever organs or appendages are in that area.

The Reiki vibration enters a person's system and gradually dissolves, layer after layer, the energy knots created by recurring thoughts and feelings of a negative nature. As this process takes place, the natural flow of a person's own vital force gets restored. In this way, balance is reestablished.

Who can use it?

Reiki can be transmitted and received by everyone. A teacher awakening or attuning your system to Reiki is an essential step for you to be able to channel this energy, which is present everywhere.

You do not need great knowledge in order to use it. The "attunement," the awakening of this skill, is all you need in order for Reiki to start flowing through you every time you wish to use it. From then on your hands hold an injection of vital force that you will be able to apply to yourself or to other people, to every living thing.

Do I need to be particularly sensible in order to use Reiki?

Sensibility and capacity are two different subjects. Every person has the ability to use Reiki. Some people will be more sensible than others, which does not affect the results since we are using a technique that works, regardless of your sensibility or even of your belief in the method´s workings. Once the skill is awakened the vital energy starts flowing through you, and all you need do is to practice it and become aware of the results.

What are the effects of Reiki treatments?

Reiki prompts deep relaxation. It brings about inner meditative states, releasing any excess of mental activity, which results in a balancing of the emotions.

How is this possible? We said that Reiki is high frequency energy, identical to the vibration of Love. When it comes in contact with lower and more dense energy frequencies, it affects them. For instance, if I am resonating with an excess of anger, rage, or frustration, the vital light that a treatment transfers to my system raises the frequency of the anger, rage, or frustration energies, transforming them into higher, more positive feelings.

Should an ailment exist, Reiki may alleviate pain. It will act strengthening the energy of all areas where illness manifested, which in time will be a factor in restoring health and wellbeing to those areas.

What does one feel as he or she does Reiki?

We are talking about a light of a very subtle vibrational frequency, although its effects are not subtle at all. There is a wide scope of possible sensations you might experience as you practice Reiki.

Relaxation and wellbeing are the most frequently experienced feelings during a treatment, whether it is done upon yourself or another. A very deep compassionate or affective mood may arise because such a high degree of this energy (which is not different from love) is circulating through your whole being. Therefore, as you convey Reiki you are also receiving it.

Within your hands, you may feel warmth, a light sense of density, or a waterlike sensation over your palms. It can be described as a spiral movement pulsing as concentric circles, emanating from the very center of your palms.

In some situations, there is so much vital force concentrated in your hands that physical sensation is lost and you experience only an intense energy there, erasing the apparent boundaries between your hands and the receiver´s skin.

Sometimes you may feel prickles on your palms, or they may feel stiff, both being signals that the patient's area underneath your hands is suffering a blockage or a lack of his own vital energy.

The Reiki practice is a delightful experience for the practitioner, who is acting as a transmitter of so much vital energy resonating at the vibrational frequency of love. If you remember how important it is to find a comfortable posture as you perform a treatment, you will enjoy it so much that you will not want it to end.

What is the feeling when receiving a Reiki treatment?

A Reiki treatment brings about a very deep state of relaxation, similar to receiving several massages. On a mind level, profound silence and stillness are brought forth, and therefore the emotions become balanced.

It is possible that you feel the movement of energy throughout your body as well as a soothing sensation of warmth. You may perceive light sparkling or a waterlike density over some areas. You may witness immense love, peace, or protection unfolding from within yourself.

As you still your mind, you contribute to a deeper Reiki experience. In this sense, it is important that the Reiki practitioner directs the receiver toward a relaxed state of mind, so that both are aware of the present moment throughout the treatment. This will enable a keen awareness of subtle insights and perceptions.

Therefore, the attitude is also important. The Reiki practitioner can provide a silent atmosphere and show you how to relax your own mind, but no one other than yourself can stop your thoughts should you choose to let your mind flow unrestrained. It is the responsibility of both the practitioner and the receiver to allow the mind to steep in silence and stillness so that both enjoy a profound Reiki experience.

How long does it take to learn Reiki?

It takes ten minutes and a whole lifetime. The activation process known as "attunement" takes a total of ten to fifteen minutes. This is the only essential step for Reiki to start flowing through you. At the attunement, the intense Reiki transmission from the teacher to the student opens up certain energy channels within your system that will allow Reiki to flow from then on, every time you wish to make use of it. Yet, a whole lifetime is required to understand the deeper outcomes of using and infusing this vibration of light/energy.

This Reiki method is currently available to anyone who wants to learn it. It was not so in ancient times, since it was reserved only for individuals who had proven themselves to be loyal depositaries for such a powerful technique, those who lived an extremely healthy and disciplined life. Although our current culture does not always allow for such a lifestyle, now is the time for many people to benefit from these lifeforce injections.

This is the reason why the Reiki learning process is now divided into four grades or courses. Right after the first grade, you can enjoy wonderful results from the treatments. The second and third grades include a selection of energy symbols that "widen out" the channel already open within you. Then, you are able to pass on a greater Reiki flow. Your skill becomes heightened and you go deeper into the essence of this energy. The fourth grade is the Teachers Training, which offers a final attunement that allows you to activate in others the capacity to use Reiki.

There is an attunement for each Reiki level that considerably enhances the vibration of your whole system. It balances all the energy centers, strengthening the flow of your own vital force. You go through a transformation so profound that several days are needed for your system to become accustomed to its new and improved vibration. This is one of the reasons why the current Reiki education and attunement is divided into four steps; although we may not be able to maintain the austere and disciplined lives of the first Reiki practitioners, we can harmoniously assimilate each step of the process while living in our modern world.

I just took a Reiki course. If I do not practice it, can I lose the ability to use it?

It is said that once your capacity to convey Reiki is awakened, you never lose it. For instance, you might take a course and then never practice Reiki again until, twenty years later, you remember that you once took a course. Then the moment you place your hands with the intention to transfer this energy, Reiki will flow through you, even though you have not made use of the technique in all those years.

Of course, if you had practiced Reiki during those twenty years, you would now transmit that lifeforce with much greater potency and effect. As Reiki is practiced, it permeates the whole system, transforming our energy until it gradually vibrates on frequencies closer to the vibration of the Reiki energy. With practice, it becomes easier for us to channel this energy because it finds fewer obstacles within us; there is no kind of energy dissonance.

Can a person use Reiki, although she has never taken a Reiki course?

Whenever we feel pain, we instinctively place our hands over the affected area. As our natural warmth pours forth from the palms and our *ki* (vital force, lifeforce, *prana*, *chi*) is infused into the area, the discomfort is at least partially alleviated. Nevertheless, in order to convey the tremendous Reiki flow that a treatment allows for, it is essential to take a course and go through the attunement process.

Through various means (most of them tremendously arduous), it might be possible for a person to achieve the opening of energetic channels that allow for energy to be transmitted to another. However, without the intense transmission of the vital energy that takes place from the teacher to each student during the attunement period of the course, knowledge and understanding of the complete process is not likely to be possible, and the person's effectiveness will be limited to what he or she can discover on their own. Therefore, taking a course is the easiest and most effective way and a wonderful option.

I heard there is a twenty-one-day purification process following the Reiki attunement. Can you please explain what that means?

The overall energy of each person who comes to a course "vibrates" at a certain frequency, depending on how healthy her body is and the way she thinks and feels. The Reiki transmission at the attunement session is so hugely powerful that it actually refines our own energy, enhancing it and bringing its vibration closer to the loving pulsation of Reiki. This dramatic transformation of our own energy would be impossible for us to integrate in only one day, and it is beneficial that it takes place more gradually over approximately three weeks.

In order to facilitate this process, it is recommended that students look for tranquility and avoid unrestrained behaviors. As we leave the course we enjoy a brand new energy full of peace and stillness; for the following twenty-one days our vibrational frequency might go up and down in a harmonious flow until, after about twenty-one days, it finally settles at the highest level it reached at the time of attunement. From that day on, it will stay at the attunement level.

For this reason and as a result of this energy adjustment, it is possible to find oneself in an extremely sensitive mood: We might find the emotions to be altered for no apparent reason, or we might feel a deep affection and compassion toward everything and everyone around us. This is all a natural part of coming into harmony with the new energetic frequencies.

Do I need to have faith in Reiki in order to enjoy wonderful results?

Reiki is a technique that works once the skill has been awakened. It does not depend at all on faith or on how much we believe we can attain with it. Since we are talking about an energy that is not visible, we might think that faith is needed in order to best make use of it. However, this is not the case. We cannot see electricity, but we know it works; we do not see the radio waves, but we know they convey information. All that is needed in order to make use of the electrical energy and the radio waves is a transmitter and a receiver becoming attuned to the same frequencies. The same is true of Reiki.

If you were to take a Reiki course and believed not a single word of what you were taught, and then were to actually practice the technique and follow the steps that were given (even while doing it with an attitude of absolute unbelief), you would find that the vital force would inevitably flow through your hands with a great intensity, whether or not you had "faith" in it. Of course, in order to test the results for yourself, you must practice it.

Can I cause harm with Reiki?

If Reiki were to consist of a massage or a potion preparation, we could hold doubts about its effects since we could make mistakes during the massage or the preparation of the potion. However, when performing a Reiki treatment and simply placing our hands over certain areas of the body, there is no pressure or movement. As a great amount of Reiki is transmitted, vital force and love permeate both the practitioner and the receiver. For this reason there is no possibility for harm.

Let us consider the case where the receiver might be holding an intense emotional burden on a subconscious level, causing an energy blockage within his or her system that (since the physical manifestation has not come about yet) remains unknown to them. When performing a Reiki treatment in this case, there are two possible reactions that could take place:

- ☙ The area affected by the energy blockage is infused with vitality. As we start moving a numb leg we feel some pain because the blood circulation is being reactivated. In the same way, as the energy flow is reactivated through an area where it had remained blocked, it is possible to experience some pain or discomfort. The muscles might even "vibrate" as a result of the energy movement.

- ☙ There can be a negative emotional response and the person being treated might wonder why Reiki "makes me feel this way." The answer abides in the fact that as any emotional burden stored within the subconscious mind is released, it has to be seen—it must be exposed before it can be expelled—and there are no exceptions to this. Nevertheless, great inner freedom follows such a process and, in this way, real inner transformation takes place.

It is important that we come to understand the reasons why these reactions take place, and know that they are actually very positive since they are bringing forth a greater freedom within us. The truth is that either the energy blockage or the emotional burden could stay untouched; however, within a few years they might be the underlying reason for an illness, once our system is no longer able to hold a weakened energy flow. We allow for a positive transformation as we let the process unfold, understanding the basis of what is really taking place.

I enjoy good health. What do I need Reiki for?

Although Reiki is often described as a "healing" technique, you do not need to be ill or in pain in order to take a course or receive a treatment. Its effect is always beneficial.

One of Reiki´s attributes is that its energy vibrates at the same frequency as love. The deepest essence of each human being is love. Why, then, are we unaware of this? One reason is the tremendous mental activity that goes on within our minds; it keeps our focus on the constant images that thoughts give rise to, reinforcing our belief in being limited and imperfect individuals. This is so far away from our deepest and true essence: infinite and universal love.

With so much noise going on in the mind, it is not easy to realize our true essence, although it is always present whatever we do; it is a state beyond the emotions that arise from thoughts. We usually live our reality at the mental level, which is one of the most superficial layers of our being.

The purpose of any work regarding our inner growth is to destroy our false beliefs, to cleanse our mind of any limiting thoughts so that we may come to realize our great innate freedom and our deepest nature.

For instance, someone who starts a Reiki practice due to a health issue will first find balance on a physical, mental, and emotional level. This is the first step to fully allow for our inner development. Once this equilibrium has been attained, the next movements that Reiki impels have to do with a harmonious release of those tendencies that keep us limited or that cause us to hold on to any unwanted emotional burden.

In this way, our energy is gradually transformed and attuned to the qualities of love. And for this reason, Reiki is always beneficial.

Why does Reiki reduce stress?

Reiki reduces stress because it helps to restore balance on all levels: physical, mental, and emotional. It releases muscular stiffness, providing the physical body with deep rest. It brings forth inner meditative states, bringing relief to the mind. As the mind finds rest, the emotions, which are a direct consequence of our thoughts, become still. Any excess of unwanted emotions is softened by the loving sensation that a Reiki treatment creates within us.

If you have already taken a Reiki course, you may want to do treatments on yourself at night, while you are falling asleep. The hands placed on your body – until you naturally change your posture – convey enough vital energy to provide a deep and restorative sleep. Sometimes you will wake up in astonishment at your overflowing vitality and wonderful mood, and you will know that you fell asleep while your hands kept pouring Reiki all night long.

Is it possible to do so much Reiki that I get "saturated" with it?

It is never too much. Even if we were to fall asleep doing Reiki on ourselves to wake up the next morning realizing it has been pouring into us all night long, it can never "saturate" our system; or, rather, a system that is saturated with vital force is in perfect balance.

Let us imagine that we have already done so much Reiki on ourselves that we are perfectly balanced. Once Reiki restores our physical, mental, and emotional balance, it starts working on the limiting mental and emotional impressions held within the subconscious mind, and gradually brings about deeper states of peace, freedom, and wellbeing. Since the energy of Reiki is in fact one with our own deepest energy of loving awareness, the more "saturated" with it we become, the more we will experience this transformation of our very being.

Since I took a Reiki course I want to be a better person

This usually happens at our very first contact with Reiki. First of all, the experience of the attunement helps us perceive that we are not only a physical body: a significant realization that transforms many concepts about ourselves and our life.

On the other hand, this also wakes us up to a greater awareness regarding that which we truly are, the true purpose of our life, and the ways in which we impact our environment. All our actions, our true intentions, our thoughts, and our words constantly affect everything and everyone around us, whether we realize it or not.

For instance, we may unconsciously hurt others and justify whatever pain we create; we can even perform actions that will have a negative impact on us in the future. However, as a person taps into the energy realm – which happens every time we use Reiki—she becomes more and more aware of the real impact of her own presence. As she realizes that on an energy level there is an underlying unity between all and everything, she understands that harming another is hurting someone whose essence is not different from her own. Regardless of the other person´s personality or faults, his essence is love. Also, she comes to know that in hurting another she is creating pain that will come back to her in the future.

For this reason, we may suddenly realize that we held and justified unwanted tendencies for a long time that now, due to our heightened awareness, have no value since we are looking for a greater harmony in our lives.

Or, because we understand the impact of our very presence upon our environment, we wish to act in ways that resonate more with affection and therefore we want to be a better person.

> ***I practice Reiki on a regular basis. Since I've been doing it, the answer to difficult situations in my life naturally arises within me.***

This is a similar instance to the previous one. As we practice Reiki our Consciousness is heightened and our mind becomes still. For this reason, it is easier for us to "listen" to innate wisdom that arises from within in the way of insights and clear answers to certain circumstances. We hold great resources within that we can benefit from as we supply our mind with the rest it needs.

Ever since I took my first Reiki course I feel calmer. Things do not affect me so much.

This happens a lot to people who take their first Reiki course. There are two reasons for it:

- Reiki starts a process of dissolving impressions (thought and behavior patterns) that we held within which, up to now, made us react automatically to certain outer stimuli. As such reactions lose their strength, we may still go through similar situations but they no longer affect us since there is no reaction to them.

- Every time we practice Reiki we are filling ourselves up with love. Actually, the intensity of Reiki poured into us during the attunement dramatically enhances the quality of our energy. This triggers calm and stillness in us, and therefore outside situations do not affect us so much.

THE LAYERS

OF A HUMAN BEING

AND THE EFFECT

OF THOUGHTS

The Layers of a Human Being and the Effect of Thoughts

For the sake of a deeper understanding of the Reiki *modus operandi*, it may be useful to broaden our perspective of who we really are, so that our new vantage point may help us resolve any doubts regarding the effects of a treatment.

Eastern philosophies explain that a human being is not only the physical body that we touch and see. They view a person as a series of layers superimposed upon one another. First we find the physical layer, the physical body. In this chapter we will take into consideration the second layer: our "body of light" or energy layer.

Buddhists explain the physical body as being the "gloves" and the energy body "the hands" that, as they enter the glove, animate it. Without the energy body, the physical body remains inert.

Our energy channel system

The heart impels our blood circulation through the veins and arteries throughout our physical body. In the same way, there is a whole system of subtle arteries, or energy channels, throughout our energy body. Our vital energy, also called *prana, ki,* or *chi* circulates through them.

There are millions of these channels distributed all throughout our energy body. The main and most important one extends from the base of the spine through the crown of the head. Along this channel we find the seven wheels, or *chakras*, whose function is to impel our vital energy, in the same way that our heart pushes our blood in order to deliver it throughout our body. There are *sub-chakras* in some other locations, such as the palm of our hands or feet.

Energy channels meet at each *chakra* and in this way, everything within us is connected.

Our thoughts and feelings are forms of energy

Everything that exists is a form of energy. For instance, the difference between objects or substances such as the floor and milk, or a stone and a feather, lies in the frequency of vibration of their particles. This makes the various substances take on different energies. For instance, particles of a wooden table vibrate on a lower and denser frequency than particles within water, which is a "softer" material of a high and faster vibrational frequency.

Each thought always gives rise to a feeling. A negative thought producing a feeling such as rage vibrates on a slow, heavy frequency. A positive thought producing a feeling such as joy, is of a faster, lighter frequency, coming closer to the vibration of love, which is simply the name given to the highest and lightest vibration that exists. Therefore, positive feelings resonate with love.

Does the energy of our thoughts and feelings affect our physical body? Do positive thoughts and feelings affect us in the same way as negative thoughts and feelings?

Maybe just an unwanted thought does not dramatically influence us. However, our tendency to continuously repeat negative thoughts and feelings, or the deep impact of a traumatic experience that triggers a corresponding emotional response, do leave an imprint within.

The energy blockages

Forms of energy of a dense vibrational frequency may accumulate in our system as we repeat them (with our thoughts and feelings). As time goes by, such residue builds up and becomes an obstacle to the free flow of our own vital energy; once it is no longer able to flow through alternative ways, the energy flow through that specific area slows down or it may even stop, becoming a blockage. Before long, an illness comes into being.

There are many different techniques that restore the energy flow within a human being. Reiki is a powerful example of one of them. As the Reiki life energy fills up the area in which the energy was "asleep," or "blocked," physical recovery can occur over time and with a course of treatments. In this way, Reiki restores balance on a physical level. Balance on a mental and emotional level is also restored as that lighter energy affects the denser vibrations in our system: If we are vibrating with too many unwanted thoughts and feelings, Reiki enhances and transforms them into more positive elements because of its own positive vibrational nature.

Reiki does not influence personality or beliefs. It simply calms any excessive display of thoughts and feelings of a negative nature. As a result, the person recovers her natural enthusiasm, her joy, her peace and bliss. She regains some of the sensations she had when she was a child and her energy flow was optimum.

Commonly speaking, we can say that one of the main functions Reiki performs is one of "cleaning out the pipes" in our system, to dissolve the energy blockages that keep our vital energy from freely flowing through our net of energy channels.

I have treated myself with Reiki for a month and a half. During one of the treatments, a vivid memory of my traffic accident suddenly came up. Why did something like this happen?

This person went through two identical traffic accidents within a year and a half. At both of them, her car was crashed into from behind by another car, and both times she was diagnosed with a cervical injury. As she describes the second accident, she explains how she lost control of the vehicle as it began spinning around. She thought, *I am dying!* And she firmly believed her time had arrived.

The car stopped; as she realized she was alive and well, at first she did not dare to turn her head to check on her children, who were traveling in the back seats. Fortunately they were unhurt.

As time went by, since her symptoms resulting from the accident did not change, she was diagnosed with fibromyalgia. A few years later she came in touch with Reiki. She was *attuned* and started doing treatments on herself every night.

The interpretation to these reactions is based on the introductions to each chapter of this book, on meditation experiences as well as on Eastern philosophies. It is worthwhile to contemplate the effect of our own thoughts and feelings upon our physical system, and thankfully there already exist several studies in this regard.

One night, while doing Reiki on herself, she sees her last accident very vividly. She is disturbed by the emotional intensity and clarity of her perception. Her recovery had continued ever since she first began using Reiki, and now she cannot understand why she is "seeing and feeling" such a traumatic event once again.

The intensity of the real accident evoked the thought *I am dying!* followed by a lurid emotional discharge. Although she soon realized that no one had died, her cells had already absorbed the "I am dying!" message. And, most importantly, they started resonating with it. Responding to the intensity of that feeling, the cells soon generated a degenerative and mortal condition.

We can see how this process takes place in an unconscious way and on a cellular level. No one wants to become sick and, in most cases, we fail to reflect on the real, deep-seated causes when we do.

As Reiki is applied, it acts upon *the source of the imbalance,* which in this case was the firm belief that death was about to occur. Reiki expelled the affirmation *I am dying!* from her system so that her cells became free from it and she was able to recover her health.

During that one treatment, she realized the deep impression she had assimilated into her system at the accident. When an impression, a belief, is expelled from within the subconscious mind, we have to see it—to be expelled, it must first be exposed. There is a time of intense emotional charge and then the experience of great freedom and wellbeing.

Why are the results of Reiki treatments different on two people who suffer the same illness?

Let us consider that, due to an illness, a person decides she wants to receive Reiki treatments. Both she and the therapist ignore the history of thoughts and emotions that created the imbalance. When two people suffer the same ailment, their personal histories differ, as does their attitude toward recovery.

For instance, one of them holds a bigger emotional burden than the other, and she affirms her ailment is chronic. The emotional burden within the second person is not as severe, and she firmly believes in her own recovery. As Reiki is transmitted, the same quantity of vital energy enters each one. However, it needs to "cleanse out" a greater volume of wounding emotions stored within the first person, so it might take more time and treatments for her to feel relief.

Our idea of recovery is also very important. Who or what is able to help someone who does not believe her healing is possible? A Reiki treatment injects vital force, and right then the patient feels relief. However, if she displays her firm belief on the illness' perpetuity, she enlivens such a fact and makes it real in her experience once again.

On the other hand, the moment we are able to visualize ourselves in perfect health, we are greatly adding to the work of Reiki, since that open attitude helps us to understand what thoughts and attitudes created the imbalance, and it helps us to transform them.

I am negative about this situation. I cannot think otherwise!

As we face what we consider to be an unwanted situation, our reaction is often of the same nature. However, every time *we allow* such a response, negative emotion is discharged through our system. Being aware that we are the ones who create and hold thoughts in our mind, we can make the effort to change our perspective in order to feel better. We can *chose to replace* the train of negative thoughts and feelings, creating and putting our attention on a more positive perspective of the situation that we are facing.

This attitude will also add to the effects of Reiki. If the person receiving Reiki takes advantage of the deep peace that she taps into, and she acts upon the insights she will gain regarding the cause of her illness, Reiki will have a greater effect. In this way she will be able to transform those attitudes or thought patterns which, repeated over time, affected the free flow of her own vital energy.

In all cases Reiki will permeate the system of the person receiving a treatment. Nevertheless, it cannot force someone to change the patterns of thoughts or emotions. It is always up to the receiver to decide whether he or she accepts transformation.

For many years my life was difficult and I suffered greatly. How can Reiki help me?

Suffering exists because of ignorance—a lack of knowledge about our greater potential and about that which is truly taking place behind the circumstances that life brings forth into our experience. At difficult times our tendency is to allow unwanted thoughts and feelings to run rampant.

Thought is the great creative force; it acts as a magnet attracting to us circumstances equal to the essence of the thoughts we entertain. This is why, as we focus on unconstructive thoughts:

- ๑ We keep attracting the same corresponding emotions, situations, and circumstances again and again, perpetuating in our lives that which we are not fond of.

- ๑ A harmful, toxic energy is released throughout our system, obstructing the free flow of our own vital force and resulting in poor health.

As we learn Reiki and apply it to ourselves on a regular basis, our system becomes infused with a vibrational frequency of light that is one with love. Even with the first treatment we enjoy deep inner stillness and rest. This love vibration also diminishes the intensity of any negative thought patterns. Now we are resonating in a different way. Therefore, the creative force of our thought, which is constantly operating, starts attracting fewer unwanted circumstances and begins to attract, or project, only positive ones. Reiki affects our *vibrational frequency* (our "vibe"), which is always and ultimately the cause of all situations that we attract into our lives.

At the same time, Reiki is dissolving any residue from old emotional patterns that were created by the ways we interpreted the situations and circumstances of the past.

We begin to enjoy a greater harmony within, which results in greater harmony in our circumstances and relationships. Certain patterns of thought and feeling are immediately dissolved, while others that we might have been feeding for months, even years, can take more time and treatments to transform. A clear *intention* to change our life is also essential.

When I received a Reiki treatment, I felt as if I were floating in the air.

This is a very common sensation. A Reiki treatment takes us deep into a very peaceful state. Surrounded by that silence, we become keenly aware of our energy body, or energy layer.

Our energy body permeates and animates the physical body and radiates beyond our skin to surround us with an egg-shaped body of light. It coexists with the physical body and whatever happens to the physical body affects the energy body (and vice versa).

This is not meant to scare anybody. To go into the energy body consciousness and to feel that floating sensation is an extremely pleasant experience, and one would never wonder, Have I left my physical body somewhere? There is the certainty that the physical body is still here and, at the same time, there is a greater awareness of the energy layer. Because this layer is composed of light, it is experienced as a weight-free, undefined field, giving the feeling of floating in the air.

Lost in our thoughts, we may not see a friend walking by; fascinated upon some image, we may not realize someone is talking to us. This does not mean that everything around has disappeared from existence: it is just that our attention is focused on something else and we do not perceive the person or the things that are right in front of us. This is exactly what happens when "we feel as if we were floating." At those times, our attention is more aware of our energy body, although the physical body "is still here." Tapping into these levels of consciousness helps the physical body to rest deeply.

As I received Reiki and my eyes were closed, I saw color shades within.

This is not your imagination, since these glimpses are so bright. You are able to see your body of light when you attain enough silence in your mind, which is the same as being in meditation. As we said, your energy body is similar in shape to the physical body, and it radiates light. The energy wheels, or chakras, within the energy body may also be visible while in deep meditative states.

I felt so grateful during the Reiki treatment!

The silence and stillness that we dive into as we receive a Reiki treatment are a portal into the deeper layers of our being. We may, for instance, realize worthwhile aspects of our own essence; we may feel deep love or peace. Gratitude results from such inner recognition. Great resources within us support our freedom and fullness.

I suffer from anxiety, and it became more intense during the Reiki course. I felt anguish within my chest.

The Reiki transmission that takes place in the course remarkably transforms our overall energy. For anxiety to be worked upon, the thought and feeling patterns that support it must be broken up, for they are the cause of anxiety. As we receive so much Reiki during the course and we "push" our system into resonance with a frequency closer to the vibration of love, the rigid thought and feeling structure begins to weaken. Anxiety seems to get more intense as we become aware of the emotional intensity being expelled; however, over time, it will diminish until it is completely washed from our system.

It is interesting to consider that such reaction is taking place when we have taken no pills at all, just as a result of a Reiki treatment or an attunement.

Regular treatments are needed to move this process forward. The "anguish" sensation is due to anxiety having affected our own energy flow and therefore it affected the movement of energy through several chakras; one of them is the heart chakra, located in the center of the chest. At this particular spot, as the chakra and the "shell" covering it begin to open up, we might feel something similar to an anguish sensation or even a very physical impression that something is being unlocked.

I am surprised at watching how my heart chakra seems to close up when I think negatively, and open up when I think positively.

There is a very easy exercise we can use to prove the immediate effect of our own thoughts upon our energy. Two people and a pendulum are needed. Instead of a pendulum you can use a simple necklace with a pendant heavy enough to keep the necklace straight.

This is the exercise: One of you lies down. The other holds the pendulum about 8 inches above the center of your partner´s chest. This is the place where the heart chakra is located. The pendulum hangs still from your quiet hand. Just observe how in a few moments the pendulum starts a spiral movement, pushed by the energy that the chakra is projecting. A circling spiral movement means the chakra is open. A straight movement indicates that the chakra is blocked at that time.

For this experiment, the person lying down will close her eyes and for three minutes she will bring a negative and painful memory to mind. For another three minutes she will think of a very positive and happy memory or future mental projection. She will silently choose which one goes first.

The person holding the pendulum will observe its movement, checking when it turns straight, signal of the chakra energy being blocked, and when it turns spiral, showing that the energy flow is optimum.

As they share together after the exercise, they can prove the relationship between positive thoughts and the opening of the energy flow and negative thoughts and the blockage of the energy flow.

When I do Reiki treatments on others, I like to take on a meditative attitude and to perform them in silence. I totally lose any sense of time and I feel so fulfilled that I do not want the session to end.

This is the ideal attitude to take on by a Reiki practitioner. We can all take a course and convey vital energy from then on. However, the result of treatments depends in a great measure on our attitude as we perform them.

As we treat someone else, all the Reiki entering the other person is passing through us, and therefore it is filling us up as well. If we are able to keep a meditative open-eyed state, we allow for mental silence and this is when the flow of Reiki reaches its highest intensity.

Any desire for a successful treatment, any worry about whatever is or is not taking place within the receiver means tension, and this tension obstructs a high Reiki flow. Therefore, the best attitude is one of silence, open-eyed meditation, and detachment concerning the possible results.

Reiki itself stimulates inner meditative states and they will be deeper if we consciously allow for such states while we do a treatment. It is because of the mental stillness we attain that we lose track of time; as a result, the enormous peace we feel restores the physical body. Any person receiving a treatment from a Reiki practitioner who takes these suggestions into account will enjoy a very deep experience and better results in a shorter frame of time.

Can I affect my own thinking and use Reiki in order to think more positively?

Thought is a creative force. Our habitual thought processes are literally shaping all the circumstances that come into our experience. This is happening all the time, whether we are aware of it or not.

We were born thinking positively, this is our innate tendency. As we grow up this faculty may be forgotten if we have been taught to negatively project our thoughts in regard to certain subjects and circumstances.

Regular Reiki treatments mean we are bathed in light. This light affects any excess of negative vibration resonating in us as a result of our thinking. As this light vibrating as love stills the mind and brings about meditative states, we are able to regain our natural tendency to think and feel positively. And it is important to always take responsibility for the quality of thoughts that we allow to permeate our system at any given moment.

When I have a recurring unwanted thought, how can I use Reiki in order to get rid of it?

Thoughts do not disappear just because we decide we want to get rid of them. We need to turn the light on in order to get rid of darkness and the same happens with our minds: we need to "turn on the light" of a new thought in order to erase another.

Although the process I am about to describe is the same without using the Reiki technique, doing so brings serenity and joy in us, which are wonderful ingredients to help and stimulate the procedure.

Once we are aware of the recurring thought, we can use any time of stillness to reflect upon what it is that we would like to think and feel instead. We will look for a present and positive statement; then we will do brief Reiki treatments of about 20 minutes long, touching the forehead chakra and silently repeating that sentence. A positive affirmation such as "I create only positive and uplifting thoughts, which causes my moment-to-moment experience of life to unfold in positive and uplifting ways."

Daily treatments will be needed until we realize the thought we wanted to transform has become almost nonexistent and the one we chose as a substitute is now familiar to us.

At first, it is normal to feel a "shocking effect" since both ideas, which are contrary to each other, are very active in us. At this initial stage, it is important that we adopt the attitude of "ignoring the evidence of the senses." The thought pattern that we are dissolving is still projecting certain negative situations upon the screen of our life, while at the same time we are consciously holding in our mind its opposite thought and feeling! This will last for a short period of time, until the automatic emotional reaction that we are working on loses its momentum, and our circumstances change in a harmonious way to fit the positive statement that we have begun resonating with.

TREATMENTS

ON ONESELF

Treatments on Oneself

In order to be able to apply Reiki to oneself and to other people, it is essential to take a course where a teacher activates this skill. All of us have certain healing skills and some warmth is always poured through the palms of our hands. However, this is very different to the process taking place as a person applies Reiki, where energy is projected with the same intensity as a waterfall. It is an extremely bright light which fills up the whole body the moment the practitioner´s hands rest on any spot.

Reiki is everywhere. It is the essence and support of everything alive. As we learn how to use it, we can fill ourselves up with energy every time we do a treatment on ourselves or others.

Reiki is a very easy method and all you need is an attunement for it to start working. You do not need to learn difficult techniques. As soon as you want to let it flow through you, all you need to do is to activate the Reiki stream with your intention.

Many people come to the courses because they want to learn Reiki just to do self-treatments. For them to get the highest benefit from Reiki, a twenty-minute treatment every day will be needed, although one daily hour would be ideal.

We can use Reiki on ourselves as a tool for relaxation and stress reduction; to help us rest, to fill ourselves up with vitality, to keep a state of optimum health, or to recover from an illness. Every treatment fills us with peace and balance. In time we start noticing changes in our attitude, as things do not affect us so much; we feel more stillness and joy and we are able to contribute to the harmony of our environment. We radiate a special peace and we hold within ourselves a tool that we can always use when it is needed.

Receiving Reiki on a regular basis will help us face life with a relaxed attitude, respond positively to daily events, resolve emotional conflicts, and be more sensitive toward ourselves and others. This affects our circumstances in very obvious ways. For this reason, many students affirm that taking a Reiki course changed their lives, since it helped them improve their relationship with themselves and, therefore, their relationship to their environment.

I want to learn Reiki just to do self-treatments.

Doing self-treatments on oneself is highly beneficial. Many people take Reiki courses to use this method just on themselves and their closest ones. You can do as much Reiki as you want to. Little by little, these treatments balance your own energy flow and they help you rest deeply, find relaxation, and enjoy an enhanced overall vitality.

Become accustomed to doing Reiki on yourself as you fall asleep. Those few minutes of practice and transmission of vital energy allow for an optimum energy circulation and help you relax and rest. Sometimes you will fall asleep with your hands passing on Reiki; you will be amazed when you wake up earlier than usual, deeply rested and full of vitality, as in your childhood. You will see how waking up earlier does not affect the quality of your day but just the opposite, you will feel more alive, still, and joyful.

When I do a treatment on myself, should I do all of the Reiki hand positions that we learned in the course?

The hand positions that are learned first in a Reiki course are just a guide intended to help you follow logical steps, since you are just coming in touch with this subtle energy.

The most important and central aspect of a Reiki course is the attunement: a powerful Reiki transmission from the teacher into the student that activates the ability to use this energy. Of course, all the theory that follows helps you gain an intellectual understanding of this method. However, that is not a requisite for you to attain wonderful results in Reiki.

As you use Reiki, you can decide in which way you want to use it. Right after taking a course, you hold within your hands a huge shot of vital energy.

The hand positions taught in the course involve touching all of the chakras and this guarantees that you are deliberately infusing life into all of the organs close to each of those energy wheels.

Nevertheless, Reiki is light. As we turn on a light switch, the bulb holds the highest intensity of light and heat, yet the light fills every corner of the room. The same happens with your hands as you are doing a Reiki treatment: your palms hold the highest intensity of light and heat, and as soon as you place them on a single spot of the body, that light is immediately spread throughout the whole body and the vital energy is utterly permeating the receiver´s system.

The most important fact to consider while performing a treatment is the length of time we assign to a session. We cannot expect wonderful results with only a five-minute Reiki transmission. At least fifteen or twenty minutes are necessary in order to start feeling some benefits. The ideal frame of time is from forty-five minutes to one and one-half hours per treatment.

Considering this, you can decide how much Reiki you need. You may want to use it as maintenance, just to relax and reduce stress. In this case, twenty minutes a day are needed. You may want to learn Reiki because you need to restore your physical balance. In that case, at least an hour of Reiki every day will be needed, which you can complete within one or two sessions.

Is there some kind of reaction possible during or after a treatment?

It is possible that a reaction takes place. In Reiki we know reactions as healing crises. We said that either a shocking situation or harmful thoughts and feelings repeated over time may block or prevent our energy from freely flowing throughout our system. From an energy point of view, physical areas suffering from a weakened energy flow are asleep and organs nearby slumber.

A huge amount of Reiki enters the system and those areas are filled up with life. As this happens, it is possible that we feel some pain or notice energy or even physical movements.

We can easily understand this by using the analogy of sitting too long and causing a limb to "go to sleep," or become numb: As the blood circulation is activated we feel tingling or even pain. And this is exactly the way we explain any healing crisis: An area where the energy flow was blocked is filled up with vitality and because of the energy flow activation, we may feel some pain. We should just witness it with the awareness that it is a positive sensation since as it ends, we step into an improved physical balance.

An "uncontrolled" reaction will never take place, because Reiki acts upon the receiver as he or she needs and is able to assimilate it. A healing crisis is rare and it usually takes place either when people suffer a significant physical disease or hold a latent illness or an extreme emotional burden.

In most cases, a treatment brings about deep relaxation, peace, and stillness to the mind as well as wellbeing.

I do Reiki on myself every day, but I feel nothing.

If we state this, there are two questions we should consider:

- ও How long do I allow for each treatment, and how do I perform the treatment?

- ও Although "I feel nothing" during the treatment, am I aware of any change in my day or in my life?

Regarding the first question, when we start using Reiki it is essential that we allow at least forty-five minutes for our practice if we want to have any insights of this energy. That is the necessary time for our mind to relax enough so that we can be aware of the subtleties of this energy. Silence is vital, so during the treatment, please avoid distractions such as TV and conversation (real or imaginary).

However, we said that Reiki is a technique that works. This means that vital energy is coming into our system even though we may not be able to calm our mind. It is for this reason that if we allow for the time needed for a good treatment, but still affirm that "we feel nothing," we should observe our day as well as our overall life and we will appreciate the differences regarding our mood, our own inner peace, and our physical and mental balance and joy.

How much Reiki each person needs depends upon many factors. For this reason, if we observe that "we feel nothing" we should extend the time we allow for each treatment and try to create silence (within and without), paying attention to our breath and to the present moment.

I do Reiki on myself while I fall asleep and my wife, who sleeps next to me, is recovering from her back ache.

This is a very clear example on how Reiki works. The moment he activates this energy torrent, it mightily runs into him through the crown of his head. It fills up his body and it is radiated beyond his skin. The palms are the means through which Reiki is emitted with a greater intensity.

Because Reiki glows through his body, although he is not "treating" his wife, the light of Reiki is reaching her and positively affects her.

As I treat myself with Reiki, my mind becomes so active that I need to stop the treatment.

We said that Reiki acts on all levels: physical, mental, and emotional. In this case, it is interesting that the moment you start treating yourself, your mind becomes extremely active. Why is this happening? Without any Reiki treatment, your day or week would go on under intense mental activity. However, as you treat yourself, your tendency to excessively think is suddenly intensified, to then get calmer, so that you will be able to enjoy more peaceful moments than usual during your day.

As you continue to apply Reiki on yourself, this mental reaction may keep happening for some time. However, you should notice that your days are different; they are calmer regardless of the intense mental activity during the sessions. In time, you will notice that your mind becomes still because Reiki helped it get rid of the tendency to overthink.

When I do Reiki on myself at night, I rest so deeply!

A healthy person may get accustomed to doing Reiki on herself as she gets into bed at night. This is a very easy trick that will help her keep and develop an optimum energy flow throughout her energy channels, as she is applying Reiki on herself on a regular basis.

If we do Reiki on ourselves as we lay in bed at night, we will probably stay like that for a few minutes until our posture naturally changes when we fall asleep. Sometimes we will fall asleep while Reiki keeps pouring through our hands all night long, and we will notice that we wake up earlier, totally rested and alert and in a great mood, as in our childhood. Reiki allowed for a profound and restorative rest as our body relaxed very deeply and our mind became still.

Can Reiki help me get rid of stress?

Reiki is known as a method to eliminate stress because it brings about a great relaxation on all physical, mental, and emotional levels in a very short time.

When a treatment ends, the stillness is so noticeable that it is hard to come out of it and it takes some time for the patient to start moving his or her body; there is great peace and an overall sense of wellbeing. This counteracts the effects of stress and helps the person rest deeply in a very short frame of time. Of course, little by little we will need to allow for some habitual thought and behavioral patterns to change if we want the antistress effect of Reiki to last.

Doing treatments on yourself at night for half an hour while falling asleep, will soon show wonderful results. If possible, try to go for another twenty-minute session at some other point during the day.

Ever since I began doing Reiki on myself, I feel content and lighter.

This is natural, since Reiki treatments counteract any excess of unwanted mental or emotional activity, helping us to regain our innate ability to think and feel in positive ways. Of course, this triggers an overall lightness in us, in the same way that laughing a lot helps us feel lighter than diving into anguish.

What is the benefit I get from learning how to treat myself with Reiki?

The main benefit you get from learning how to treat yourself with Reiki is that you own a tool that helps you gain peace and balance, and you may use this tool on a regular basis or just whenever you need it.

If you decide to treat yourself daily, you will enhance your physical, mental, and emotional states.

You can use it during crisis as well as any time you need to regain your focus. It may be used as a self-development tool, in order to overcome limitations in the form of unnecessary thought and behavioral patterns.

Regular Reiki treatments enhance restful sleep, help us to feel joyful and light, strengthen the immune system, and helps in the prevention of future health issues.

How often should I treat myself with Reiki?

It is best to treat yourself with Reiki between half an hour and one hour every day. We can go for a full conventional treatment at some point of our day or just do a shorter version while we fall asleep at night.

A person suffering from a disease should treat herself with Reiki for at least an hour a day. She might need weeks or months of treatment in order to notice distinct improvement, although relief will be felt from the very first session.

There will never be a Reiki overload, and therefore we can receive and apply as much Reiki as we want to.

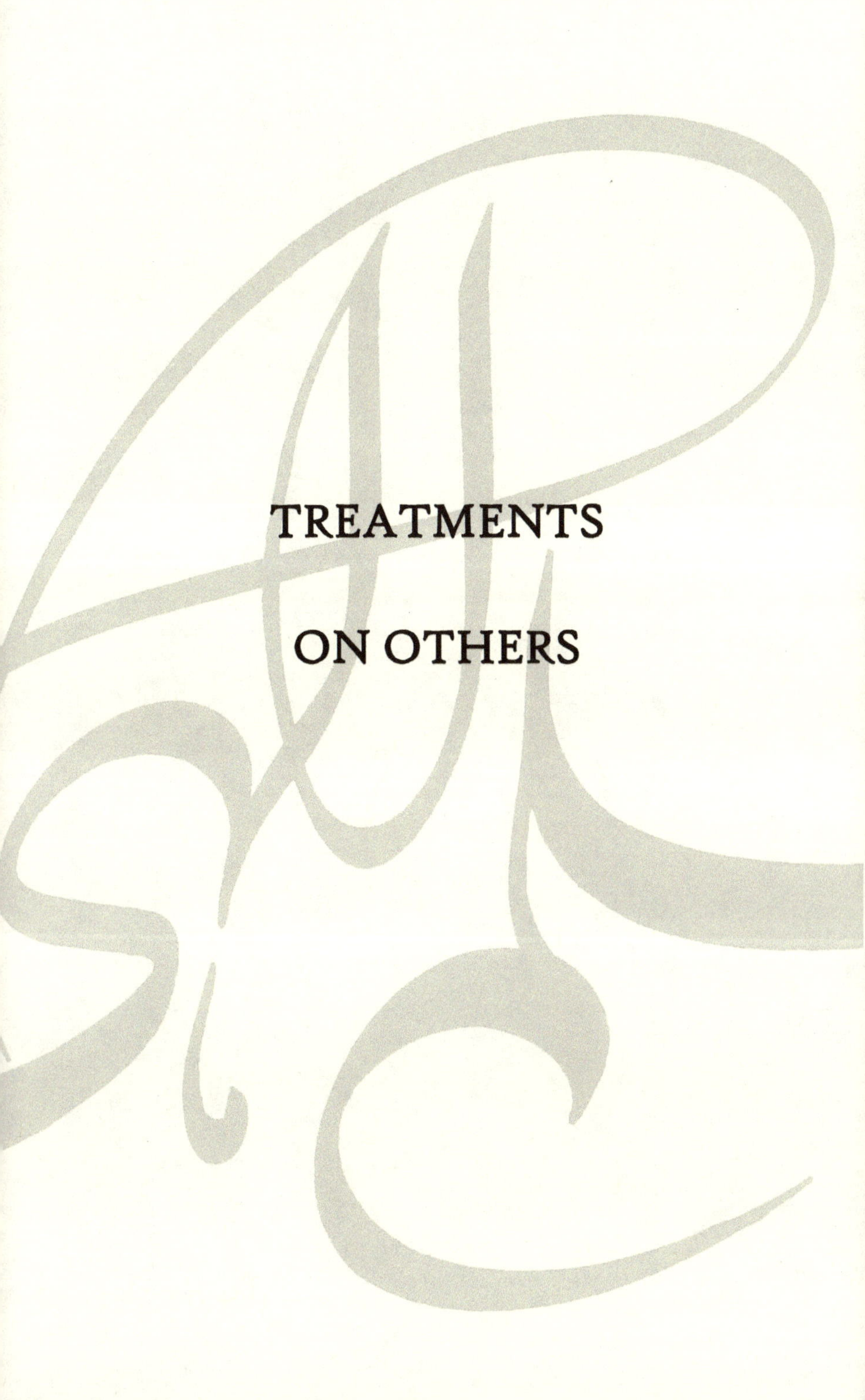

TREATMENTS

ON OTHERS

During the practice session within the Reiki course, as students get ready for their first treatment, they often feel amazed at such clear sensations of the energy running through their hands and body. It is astonishing for them that something like this happens just because they have been attuned and without the need of great efforts.

Because it is not visible, we may think of Reiki as something tenuous, almost unperceivable; maybe we picture it as a soft mist and doubt that it may have a significant effect, or we may think we need great efforts and focus to make it work. None of these beliefs are accurate.

The main focus of the Reiki course is to awaken a skill that is already innate to human beings. Also, we learn how to take the most advantage of this energy, study the steps to follow, and learn the ideal inner attitude that allows for a greater Reiki flow.

The moment we formulate the intention to perform a treatment, a Reiki lightning explodes and enters full speed through the crown of our head, and it is transmitted in the same way through the palms of our hands toward the person receiving the treatment. If we could take a picture of what is taking place from then on, we would be able to see a dense channel of white light fully covering the Reiki practitioner, "hiding him or her" within the light. So to speak, we would see a column of light and two hands and feet coming out of it.

On some occasions, the Reiki practitioners describe a light feeling of heaviness over their heads, which is due to the high concentration of energy. From then on, the range of perceptions is unlimited. The energy world is vast and rich. What a wonder it is to start the journey to explore it!

Perhaps the most rewarding time is the end of the session, when we check the effect of Reiki upon the person who received it. Reiki can be applied upon any living creature with the intention of bringing about a deep relaxation or alleviating the symptoms of an ailment.

Since we are using an energy that we do not see, this technique may be quite abstract for our own reasoning. Because it has not been fully explained by science yet, it is recommended that as we perform a treatment or talk about the method we avoid creating any esoteric atmosphere. We do not need to make complicated movements or to talk about Reiki in ways that may confuse the person hearing us, explaining things that we might not fully understand. The effects of Reiki are the best proof. When a person feels better as a result of a treatment, not that many words are needed.

Should there be a healing crisis, it is good to explain to the patient that these reactions are always beneficial and that they come up because our system is releasing unwanted negative energies and adjusting itself into a better stance. This is all we truly know. Unless the Reiki practitioner is a medical professional, he or she should not diagnose; however, if an intense reaction is experienced, you can recommend visiting a doctor.

We do not need to know how to interpret a reaction. It is enough to know that the organism is adjusting to the energy flow reactivation in an area where it had been numb for some time. The person undergoing the healing crisis will ask for another session as soon as she feels a deep recovery.

Reiki practitioners usually find their intuition heightened and they may get insights about the patient as they perform a treatment. It is very important that we are extremely respectful, careful, and discrete toward the person receiving the session. Unless we are 100% sure of the purity and truth of our perception, it is best to be discrete and avoid comments. As we said, the results of the treatment speak for themselves and anything the person needs to know will come up for her at the time needed.

When performing a treatment, if we can remember how important it is to keep an open posture with our spine elongated we will enjoy the session very much. We are receiving a full treatment while we treat someone else, because the Reiki going into the other person is coming through us.

Who can benefit from Reiki?

You can treat adults, young people, elderly people, children, pregnant women, animals or plants: Reiki benefits every living thing. There is no way to do it "wrong" and it can never hurt. When we want to do Reiki on others, it is respectful to ask their permission, if possible; however, Reiki will never do harm and can only do good.

Can I do Reiki anywhere?

Once you take a Reiki course, you hold within your hands a great injection of vital energy that you can apply to any living being. Therefore, you can do Reiki at anytime and anywhere.

Reiki reaches its highest intensity when it is transmitted through organized systems. This is a very important quality to remember about this subtle energy.

What is an organized or ordered system? To receive the full benefits of Reiki for the receiver and for yourself, you will want to consider "order" in the following areas:

ೋ **An organized system in regard to the place where the treatment is performed:** The space that you use for the treatment is neat, ordered, silent, warm, comfortable, and supports a pleasant and relaxed feeling.

ೋ **An organized system in regard to the physical body of the person receiving the treatment:** You can ask the receiver to take a posture that allows her to be comfortable during the session. You can place a cushion underneath her knees and head and slightly stretch her. Her arms should lay aside.

🕉 **An organized system in regards to the mind of the person receiving the treatment:** You can help her mind become still and release any excess of thoughts, giving her an easy meditation instruction before the treatment begins; you may start with a few deep breaths. All of this will calm the emotions, allowing Reiki to have a deeper effect.

🕉 **An organized system in regard to you as a Reiki practitioner is essential to allow Reiki to act at its highest intensity:** It is through the practitioner that vital energy is transmitted. There will be a higher quality and intensity of Reiki if your physical body is clean, free of toxins, and in harmony, enjoying order within your mind and emotions. It is for this reason that the advanced Reiki students are encouraged to maintain a meditation practice.

Anyone who takes a course will be able perform Reiki on others; and because this energy knows no limits, because it is a force whose unfoldment never ends, your ability to transmit it continues to expand as you resonate more on the vibrational frequency of Reiki.

For this reason, you will want to use whatever means are available to "purify" your own mind and emotions of past impressions that can be the source of negativity, which is of a much slower vibrational frequency. The more positive your thoughts and feelings, the more your own system resonates with the energy of love. Your personal meditation practice will provide the means to convey the highest intensity of Reiki, attaining wonderful results in a very short time. The Reiki flow is greatly enhanced when you can maintain an inner meditative stance during the treatments.

Although the energy of Reiki works anywhere, the results will be most effective and the receiver will enjoy a deeper Reiki experience if we consider order on these four levels.

If I feel nothing when I do Reiki, does it work?

With Reiki, you are using a technique that works, regardless of your perceptions as you employ it. Lack of sensation may be due to the mind being too active, with your focus straying from the present moment. It could also be that in this particular treatment Reiki is operating on levels so subtle that it is nearly impossible to perceive. Your treatments will be greatly enhanced by your own understanding that from the moment the treatment starts, a cascade of light is flowing through you at full intensity, always, with no exceptions.

Surprisingly, even at times when you think you feel nothing, the receiver is able to describe a full range or sensations. Or it may happen the other way around: The receiver felt no particular sensations while you perceived deep impressions.

When performing Reiki treatments, is it possible for me to take on "negativity" from the receiver?

As you prepare yourself to perform a Reiki treatment, you immerse yourself in a powerful, vital energy. You can envision it as a bright white cone of light of a golden hue. Entering through the crown of your head, it fills your whole body and is radiated through your pores in all directions. It is transmitted with the greatest potency through the palms of your hands. If you see yourself as having become a ball of energy, with golden white light spreading in all directions, you would not be wrong.

As you perform the treatment, you are not using your own "personal" lifeforce, but acting as a channel, a powerful transmitter of the vital energy present everywhere at all times. Your own work on yourself, such as a regular meditation practice, will assure that your own system remains strong and able to be a conduit for Reiki.

For example, if we see a watering place for cattle, picture a huge faucet there and a lot of dirt all around. We open up the huge faucet and water starts pouring forth with great potency. Should we try to introduce dirt inside the faucet with our own hands, the strength of water would continually expel the dirt out, it would not let it in. And this is exactly what happens when you do Reiki. The Reiki flow through you as you perform the treatment is so huge, it radiates out with such intensity that you cannot get in any "negativity" from the patient. The therapist who remains attuned to Reiki will not be affected by the patient's energies.

Of course, as a Reiki practitioner you are receiving as much Reiki as you are transmitting, so your system may need to go though some adjustments. If there is a dissolvable blockage in the water pipes of your home, a full stream of water will wash it away, and this is similar to what happens as we perform Reiki. The vital light is radiated through our whole body with such intensity that any negative vibration that we hold is "washed away."

In the early stages of your own practice, you might feel some discomfort (healing crisis). This process is always beneficial and the discomfort is never "because of" the negative vibration of the person receiving the treatment. As your practice matures, your own system becomes purified of the negative impressions that caused your discomfort and your ability to transmit Reiki continues to expand.

It is essential to remember that the mind is the great creative power and that your own wellbeing will be affected by your own beliefs—whether negative or positive.

When I do Reiki, sometimes I feel great love and compassion. Why does this happen?

The energy of Reiki is not different from the energy of love. This healing energy is being powerfully transmitted through you. Your own essence is also love. Every time you do a treatment you are immersing yourself in love, bringing forth your innermost essence and making it more present in your life.

Reiki also helps us be more conscious. It brings forth an awareness of compassion and helps us to recognize the underlying unity between all and everything. This recognition and acknowledgment allows deep affection and compassion to spring up from within during a treatment.

What should I do if I forget any of the steps for a treatment while performing it?

During a treatment, you are infusing vital force, so there is no wrong way to do Reiki.

The steps taught in the courses, such as the hand positions and the instructions for beginning the session and completing it, enable us to hold a keen focus and to develop ways of more completely feeling and knowing the subtle energy sensations.

In time, it will not be necessary to follow all the steps, since this work may be done in a spontaneous way, following our own intuition. To reach this inner state, a lot of practice and trust in our own inner wisdom are needed. For this reason, we start our Reiki practice following certain steps until we develop the ability to stop mental judgments and let pure insight stream forth.

In general, for any treatment at any level of practice, there are only three essential points to consider:

a) Having been attuned.

b) The length of the treatment (forty-five to seventy-five minutes or more).

c) The silence we are able to create inside and outside ourselves.

Reiki energy is ever-expanding, and our ability to attune ourselves to this life force also increases over time, with practice. Whether or not we remember all of the steps during every treatment, the essential ingredient is always our own awareness of the vital energy that is being transmitted. Reiki can do no harm, and always benefits both the practitioner and the recipient.

Can I do Reiki to a person who does not believe in it?

What is most important is that the recipient is relaxed, with an open attitude, and has given her permission to receive the treatment. "Belief" is not important. The "faith" of the receiver is not necessary. Reiki provides its own "proof" in the results. As the practitioner, it is our job to provide the environment and suggestions that will be the most conducive to relaxation and openness.

Can I do Reiki to someone who does not want to receive it?

This question often comes up during the second-level courses, as we learn how to do distance Reiki treatments. Even though we know he or she will greatly benefit from it, we should respect and accept the receiver´s decision and do Reiki only with permission.

Reiki will always act in positive ways, but an essential aspect for a lasting recovery has to do with the receiver being open to change. She needs to take advantage of such a positive impulse and go for a change, and this is something that no one can do for her. She will need to replace old ways of thinking and feeling with something more positive if she wants health to take over.

This has to be her own personal (although sometimes unconscious) choice. If there is no commitment to her own recovery, she might feel better during the session or go through a temporary recuperation, only to find that symptoms return until she is ready to make a decision to regain optimum health.

Six months before receiving a Reiki treatment, I had been diagnosed with five fibrous cysts in my breasts. During the treatment I felt something that I would describe as a "hot concrete bar" moving from side to side inside my chest. Two weeks later an echograph confirmed that the cysts were no longer there.

The most interesting aspect of this episode of feeling something similar to "a hot concrete bar" crossing her chest, is that it took place before I touched her, just for a few seconds as I was about to start the treatment.

Something similar happens during the attunement section of a course, when I am working with a group of ten to fourteen people. As I am about to start attuning the first person, the tenth one begins noticing sensations of the energy running throughout her body. How can this be so?

In that moment when a Reiki therapist or teacher formulates the intention to perform either a treatment or an attunement, the Reiki energy becomes more concentrated in the area of the individual or the group. Although the practitioner might still be preparing for the session, the energy has already begun to work on the participants.

The steps the teacher or therapist follows for attuning or performing a treatment "guarantee" a harmonized distribution of Reiki. The energy flow is acting on a deep level within all participants from the moment preparation begins for the course or the treatment.

It was the recipient's experience that in just a few seconds' time the five cysts had disappeared. Her open attitude made this possible. Reiki energy goes directly to the "root" of the imbalance, which is always an energetic structure made up of that same energy, although highly condensed and vibrating at a lower frequency. As this structure, the foundation, is dissolved, its physical manifestation (in this case, the cysts) disappears.

How many Reiki treatments can I do in one day?

There can never be an excess of Reiki. It can always operate at deeper and more subtle levels, unfolding our greatest potential. If you remain aware of your own inner state and physical needs, you can do as many treatments as you like.

Being one of the easiest holistic techniques, every time we do Reiki to someone else, we are also being filled with vital energy. The more Reiki we do to others, the more we benefit from it.

Sometimes, after several treatments, as a Reiki practitioner you may feel a slight weight over your head. This is because of the intense concentration of energy being poured through the crown of your head and throughout your body. You might sometimes even feel drowsy and dull. This is not tiredness but a profound meditative state taking place while your eyes are open and you are performing your daily activities.

Others might perceive this great stillness and quiet in you. Your own innermost state is one of great peace and silence, and you can continue with outside activities while remaining immersed in that stillness. It is highly rejuvenating and restorative to the whole system, and it is recommended that you return to that peace and stillness as often as possible during each day and stay with it for as long as you can.

DISTANCE
REIKI

During the second-level course we learn how to perform distance Reiki treatments. Even open minded people sometimes have credibility issues regarding this possibility.

How is it possible that a Reiki treatment can be equally effective at long distances (even in another part of the world)? To understand this, it is necessary to look at things from the "energy world" standpoint.

In the "physical world" we see objects and people as separate and different from us: That wooden table is over there, six feet away from me; or: That woman over there is Mary, tall and thin, and she is fifteen feet away from me. Time and distance are relevant only in the physical reality; from the perspective of the "energy world," everything is connected on an energetic level—energy permeates and pervades the physical level of existence.

Thoughts, which are an energy structure, do not stay confined within our physical body but are radiated, broadcast throughout the ethers as a "radio signal" that instantaneously reaches and causes an effect on the whole. For instance, as we intensely think of another person, the power of our intention is reaching her right away; she may suddenly think of us without any apparent reason, and she receives the essence of our purpose (consciously or subconsciously) in the same degree as our original intention.

We usually do not establish any relationship between memories popping up in our mind and someone thinking of us. Paying close attention when this happens will help us feel the difference between those times when our mind starts rolling over an idea, which then becomes a story, which then includes the memory of such person, or the times when we recall someone in particular out of the blue, without any previous mental tale.

Therefore, it is easy to understand that as we perform a distance Reiki treatment, it is not that a bright beam emerges from us, raises above clouds and crosses over continents to fall upon the person receiving our treatment; but rather, the moment we begin to "target" the receiver with our intention and the technique used to proceed on the distance, that person, wherever she may be, is infused with a high concentration of Reiki, similar to what happens during any treatment.

From an energy point of view, measurement is not the same as in the physical world. In distance Reiki we can target many people at a time, performing the treatment over a whole group, and each of them receives Reiki as if receiving a full personal treatment.

*At the practice session of the second-level course, two
fellow participants did a distance treatment on me. As a
very special energy filled me up, I felt as if my physical
body was stuck to the floor and the rest was floating
above. What a remarkable lightness!*

*Above all, I felt great happiness and an utter lack of
pain in my body, although I knew I was connected to it.*

During the practice session, two participants did a regular,
hands-on treatment on her. As they finished, they did distance
Reiki for a few minutes while seated six feet apart from her.
Although she did not know they were going to do this, she
experienced at that time that, while her physical body was
there, she also became keenly aware of her energy body. She
felt a floating sensation. This was possible because the energy
body is composed of light and radiates beyond the limits of
our skin. Going into this consciousness provides restorative
rest, being one of the deepest relaxation states we can get into.

How do I know that distance Reiki works?

Although we gain confidence after some time of practice
and experience, our mind will always bring this question up,
because from the physical perspective, it is difficult to
understand how it is that we can perform distance Reiki
treatments that always work.

Distance Reiki treatments have been done on people under
critical health conditions and results have proven to be
exceptional. We might wonder whether such positive results

would have been the same without us doing the distance sessions.

Every time we perform either a "hands on" or a distance treatment, it is good check in with the receiver to learn what he or she felt. We do not need to know the answer to everything that she describes, because the energy world is so vast that it will never stop amazing us.

The purpose of our question is for us to learn from whatever is taking place, as well as for the person to articulate what she perceived. The mind tends to forget things it cannot understand, especially in regard to subtle sensations, and it is beneficial for the recipient to verbalize those sensations.

To perform the distance Reiki treatment, set up a date and time when the receiver can focus completely on the treatment and will not be engaged in any dangerous activity, such as driving, or climbing a mountain, that would require her full attention. This will ensure a relaxed, open, and safe environment for the treatment.

Often, the optimum time to begin will be in the evening, at a time when the receiver is in bed and ready for a relaxed treatment that leads to sleep. In this case, the receiver may not be able to immediately report the effects and might need your follow up to help her distinguish the benefits of the treatment, beyond just the benefits of the relaxed and deep sleep that results.

As you perform a regular, hands-on treatment, the patient knows, before coming, how she is feeling (sad, depressed, she is in pain... whatever). You perform the hands-on session. She may not understand how it is possible that she feels better, since you only placed your hands over her. She may not believe in Reiki. However **she feels great as she leaves**. So, she makes the following connection in her own mind: "I was in pain. I came to this Reiki session which I do not understand how it works. But as I leave I feel great. So, somehow this energy thing that I do not understand, does work."

However, when you do a distance Reiki treatment, most times you will do it at night, at a time when the receiver is falling asleep. Of course the patient will also feel wonderful as a result of the treatment, but it will be difficult for her mind to make the connection. So it may happen (and it does happen) as follows: "Oh, the Reiki practitioner said she would do that energy thing on me last night... That energy thing that I do not understand. Well, I feel better this morning but I wonder if it is because of Reiki. How could that be so? I do not know... I think I feel better because I rested so deeply."

The distance Reiki worked, and students should know that it always works. They should not feel discouraged just because in some occasions the receiver does not make the connection.

Do I have to inform the receiver that I am going to do a distance Reiki treatment for her?

It is highly recommended that we inform our patient and that he tells us when it is a good time for him to receive it. The moment we start the treatment, he will feel the same as if he is here with us in a session; the only difference being that we can do a distance treatment while he is performing his daily activities. He will definitely enjoy wellbeing and relaxation sensations.

*I did distance Reiki for my eighty-year-old mother.
Her street was being repaired, she slipped and fell,
hurting her chest, legs, and hips, and she had to be in the
hospital for a few days. As she left the hospital she could
not move nor walk, and breathing was difficult for her.*

*She does not "believe" in holistic techniques, but I did
distance Reiki on her every day, two or three times a day,
and little by little she started walking and her recovery
was amazing. She got x-rays and no one could believe
her health improved so much and so fast. She even
started dancing classes and right now her health is
excellent.*

Reiki will raise a person´s health and wellbeing to the maximum she can reach for. For now, we cannot revert age, but of course we can attain a good quality of life.

"The maximum we can reach for" is a relative expression, since you may have assumed that "your sickness is forever" and think that your best is whatever you have here and now. However, many diseases labeled as "chronic" have been erased with Reiki and other holistic treatments. We can always get better.

Under the worst conditions, for instance when an organ is irreversibly damaged, Reiki can reduce pain and convey great peace and stillness. The quality of life is uplifted when we face life's challenges with a sense of peace, harmony, and serenity.

In the case we are considering, it is gratifying to witness such a recovery in a person of her age.

How much time does a distance treatment take?

A distance treatment will take you as long as a regular treatment: from forty-five to seventy-five minutes or more. If ten minutes is all you have, a little Reiki is better than no Reiki at all; however, greater benefits will be provided with a longer treatment.

When I do distance Reiki to a group, how much time do I have to apply Reiki to each of them? Can I include the whole group within just one treatment?

With distance Reiki, a treatment for each individual is not needed as we can group them all within the same session. All of them receive Reiki as if we were personally treating each of them.

We can use the distance Reiki symbol to "target" each one we wish to include in our treatment group, or we can visualize that we install the symbol on top of the whole group as we start the session.

Is a certain attitude needed while doing distance Reiki?

The only difference between a hands-on treatment and a distance treatment is that during the distance treatment we do not need to keep our eyes open. We can close them and let go, enjoying the pleasant energy sensations.

It is important that we continually bring our attention to the present moment and that we keep a clear intention. That is the signal we broadcast that, together with the distance symbol, allows Reiki to start working upon someone else, regardless of the physical space between us.

When I do distance Reiki, I feel a great flow of energy throughout my hands which then begins to lessen and disappear. Does this mean I should finish the treatment?

It is normal to feel an intense energy flow through the hands as we perform a distance treatment. It is also normal to notice a sudden change in the form of lightness and wellbeing throughout our body. This is because as we do Reiki to someone else we are acting as transmitters of this energy and we ourselves are fully receiving so much of it.

Although it may seem to us that it stops flowing, the ideal frame of time for a treatment will always be from forty-five to seventy-five minutes. The seeming lack of sensation may be because of a change in our sensibility.

Sometimes we treat someone and feel nothing special; however, that person is able to describe a whole range of energy sensations. Reiki is actually filling her system and working at such subtle levels that we cannot perceive it. She can remain aware of the energy if she has entered into a deep meditative state, so you can continue the treatment for the suggested time, unless the receiver is going through an unsettling healing crisis.

When I do distance Reiki I visualize the person who is going to get the treatment. In my imagination, I draw the symbols over the various areas where I place my hands.

This is not strictly necessary, although it is useful for us to focus our attention and our intention, and of course this helps for a greater Reiki flow.

In the distance treatment, the energy "enters" the patient all at once, and during a hands-on treatment it is entering with a greater potency in those areas where we are placing our hands.

This person´s attitude is beneficial because, as she focuses her attention in different areas of the body, her focus assures an optimum Reiki flow.

Is just one distance Reiki treatment enough?

The effect of Reiki is more tangible if there is continuity, whether we do distance or hands-on treatments. Reestablishing the optimum energy flow requires time, as does dissolving the effect of thought and behavior patterns that have been running rampant for years. From the very first treatment, a recovery is clear, and continued treatments assure that the patient will enjoy long-lasting balance.

What should I do when I finish a distance Reiki treatment?

As you finish you can ask the patient about her experience and how she is feeling now. This will help you learn so much about Reiki. In the same way, when you do several distance treatments, you can ask the receiver about her health progress or her mood. In this way, you will know whether you should continue the treatments, at the same time you witness the evolution of her condition.

Can I do distance Reiki to anyone I want?

We should always have the other person´s agreement and be respectful with her decisions. We may consider this to be a highly beneficial technique, but doing it without permission may not be respectful.

When there is a catastrophe, many people send Reiki; that is appropriate because we are helping out under critical situations where any assistance is always needed. However, when treating people around us, it is recommended that we ask for their permission in order to do a distance session.

REACTIONS

Healing crisis is the name we give to any kind of reaction that takes place as a result of a Reiki treatment. As we said, Reiki cannot hurt and there is no way to do it wrong. As the treatment is performed, Reiki fills the person completely; it "enlightens" her, saturating all of her cells with the vibration of love. Any negative resonance that it finds on its way will be "shaken" and expelled from the system; any energy vacuum will be filled up and any blockage will be unlocked.

As a result of treatments people enter into wellbeing and peaceful states and healing crises are rare; however, it is important that we know what they are just in case they take place. We need to be clear that they are always positive; a healing crisis that we cannot control will never take place. It is also good to keep in mind that in some cases it may be appropriate for the receiver to see a medical professional.

For instance, when a disease is diagnosed, such condition did not come up just a few days or weeks before the doctor tells us. A disease is the physical manifestation of knots of energy residue shaped by unwanted emotions held within for a long time. Those deposits either block or create vacuums within our own vital energy flow. When nothing is done to dissolve those residuum and they stay in our system for a long time, the time comes when the physical body cannot contain them anymore, and a physical sickness manifests.

It is possible that we feel ourselves healthy, yet we hold energy knots that would manifest in a physical illness as we grow older. As we learn Reiki and start treating ourselves, its light fills up those vacuums. Then, although we "are healthy" a healing crisis, or reaction, may take place in the form of a slight pain or discomfort, because that area is being filled up with life: The energy flow is being reactivated.

A slight adjustment movement in our body, a negative emotional burden arising because of unresolved memories, or a sudden need to cry may take place as this energy blockage is released. It is good to remember that Reiki can do no harm, and that every reaction arising as a result of a treatment is part of the adjustment and purification process.

A bookcase may look spotless until we reach the highest shelf and find it dusty. When untouched, it seems that everything is all right. The same happens as we start any inner development work. The moment we go inside and start "cleaning ourselves up," we may become aware of much more "dust" than we thought we had: unresolved emotions that we kept stored for a long time, traumatic memories, limiting ideas about ourselves, and so on. Nevertheless, although we may be surprised at our findings, we should not forget that the result of any "purification" is always a greater freedom, joy, and harmony within ourselves and therefore throughout our life.

Why did I go through an emotional reaction while I was receiving a Reiki treatment?

During a treatment it is possible that, for no apparent reason, we become aware (consciously or subconsciously) of past memories that trigger unwanted emotions.

Reiki acts upon the root of any unbalance. When an emotional burden resulting from difficult or traumatic situations gets stored within our subconscious mind, it keeps resonating in us in the form of an energy throb. In short, we might affirm that "the issue is finished" because our conscious mind is not aware of it. Then, during or after a Reiki treatment, it is uprooted and released as a negative emotion, expelling it from our system.

Colloquially speaking, we can affirm that Reiki is "cleaning out the spider webs" from our system. Should any resonance exist, in the form or a past memory of a slow (negative) vibrational frequency, Reiki shakes and expels such an obstruction from us.

Every time an emotional obstacle is being dissolved, **we have to see it,** it cannot be otherwise. But if we remember that this intense memory will last only for a few minutes and we know that it is coming up because something negative is being erased forever, we can feel gratitude for this process since it lets us gain a greater freedom; as it ends we feel different, lighter and fulfilled.

I felt a very intense pain in my stomach the first time I received a Reiki treatment. Why?

As we previously explained, sickness is the result of knots or deficiencies within our own energy flow that have been held for a long time. At this stage of energy disharmony we may not be aware of any illness, since its physical manifestation has not come yet.

It is also possible that the illness did manifest physically and the medical treatment repaired the physical injury only, without fully restituting the energy flow, leaving the innate cause of the disease latent within.

Unaware of our own energy blockages, we receive a Reiki treatment and we are surprised that we feel pain. The vital force is activating the energy flow through an area where it was either blocked or numb. Therefore, this is a very positive reaction because our own vitality is being reinforced.

Right after my first Reiki course I treated my cousin. I started and went for the first hand position touching the crown of her head. She suddenly broke into tears and we had to take a little break for her to calm down. The next day her whole body was full of pimples. What happened?

This is a very clear example of the reaction we call healing crisis. Her tears were not because of sadness or pain, but because emotions that she held for a long time were being released. And the toxins were expelled through the skin, resulting in pimples.

When such reactions take place, usually the person going through them knows they are due to emotions being liberated and her organism being cleansed. Most people will feel a great recovery after this kind of reaction, as it happened to the person that we are talking about. The practitioner can suggest seeing a medical professional as needed.

I have been treating a person who suffers a partial breaking of the crossed preceding ligament of his knee. If I do Reiki directly on his knee, the pain is too strong. For that reason, I use the basic hand postures for his thighs, calves, ankles, and feet.

Even with my hands here, far away from the damaged spot, the pain becomes very intense, so I avoid any physical contact and I let my hands float about four inches above the body.

I would like to know if I am doing this right.

This is all very positive. The pain means the inner wound is healing very fast. It is good for the receiver to endure the pain only "as much as he can." We do not want him to suffer but it is good that he lets the pain be and the process to continue for as long as he feels at ease with it.

You can explain to him that the pain is a sign that a lot of healing activity is taking place within his knee. You can also help him to become aware of any positive changes he feels after the Reiki session. Such an injury usually requires more than one session for full recovery.

As you place your hands a few inches above his skin, the Reiki transmission is exactly the same and you avoid any slight movement or pressure that can cause pain due to the keen sensibility at that area.

In some occasions, after the Reiki treatment the person who received it had fever or felt some physical discomfort. I guess this is a healing crisis. Is it appropriate to perform Reiki treatments during the healing crisis?

You can perform Reiki sessions during a healing crisis if the receiver agrees. Fever may be due to a cleansing of toxins.

The client may come to your treatment perfectly healthy, but undergoes a healing crisis on the next day. The toxins being expelled could have remained latent until years later, when his body would not be able to hold them anymore and disease would result. Any disease recently diagnosed did not show up just a few days before the doctor told us; our system has been developing it for a long time. Again, this is a positive process because he is now getting rid of something that would have troubled him in the long term.

The Reiki practitioner should never diagnose and should recommend the receiver to go to a doctor if needed. When a healing crisis occurs, the patient might at first feel alarmed at having fever or discomfort after a Reiki session. Within a few hours, though, he will feel better than he felt before the treatment, and he might notice that the pain is totally gone.

It is good that we explain this with the intention to help the client feel confident and safe because, from the perspective of the patient, it may be troubling to come to a therapist and then to feel worse. Healing crises are rare, and the most habitual response is for people to go into deep and peaceful states.

> *After my first Reiki course I felt wonderful and I did daily sessions on myself of thirty minutes each. This week I noticed how after the first twenty minutes my body does not want any more Reiki, because I feel a force pushing my hands away from my body. I actually feel very well, my hands and my body are very hot.*

That force that "pushes your hands away" does not mean that your body rejects Reiki. Actually, it is a sign that it is taking it in very well. As you do Reiki, an intense energy field is created. Your whole body is filled up with Reiki and it radiates in all directions. It is a flow cleaning up your cells, your veins, your organs, your skin, everything! You are filling yourself with Reiki, and that very same energy radiating from your body "pushes" your own hands away.

You can and you should continue to do Reiki. It can feel as though your hands were about to float. You can let this be and it may happen that your hands float a few inches above your body, as if a dense energy current was running in between your hands and your skin.

I took a yoga retreat which I enjoyed very much, but I doubt whether taking it just a week after the Reiki attunement was a good idea. It was very intense and feelings like rage or annoyance came up inside. I felt so sensitive. My mind became so active that I could not sleep for three nights. I had to stop doing Reiki for a day and a half because I felt dizzy as I did it.

Then, last night I awakened in the middle of the night and my hands were doing Reiki on myself, as if my body was asking for it.

The reaction during the yoga course is positive. In order to transform ourselves for the better, "the worst" has to be expelled from the system. The attunement together with a yoga course released old feelings stored inside. These feelings must be exposed before they can be expelled. The process might seem emotionally intense, but if you remember that the Reiki energy is dissolving and releasing blockages, you can experience gratitude that these feelings will never come up with the same intensity again.

The extreme mental activity may also be a result of your attunement and the deep transformation taking place within you. Your mind may have developed the tendency to be too active, so this temporary intensity may be a reaction where your mind gets to its highest activity level in a short time because that tendency is actually being expelled, to then go back to a natural stillness and harmony.

Sometimes at an attunement, or as you receive a Reiki treatment, the energy body may shift a little in an adjustment movement. This creates a slight feeling of dizziness, and if you pay attention you will notice that it is not the same kind of dizziness you might experience with motion sickness. It is an adjustment within the energy body. It is a natural outcome of the movement for renewal and is never harmful.

> *During the Reiki treatment some muscles slightly trembled and I felt a minor shake, although the therapist´s hands were not over the area where this was happening.*

The deep relaxing state that you go into allows your muscles to release any tension, and this takes place in the form of tics or slight shakes within the body that are actually very nice. We also feel something like this at some occasions as we are falling asleep.

The moment a therapist places his hands over the first position, for instance on the crown of the head, the light of Reiki fills up the whole body of the person receiving the treatment. For this reason, it is working upon many different areas on various levels, regardless of where the hands of the Reiki practitioner are placed.

> *Why did I cry during the Reiki treatment?*

On some occasions, a Reiki treatment might bring on weeping as a result of a deep recognition within yourself. This is not because of sadness. As your mind finds silence you enter a meditative state that allows you to feel your deeper essence; this is very comforting and exciting.

The person I am treating affirms that she is never able to relax. However, during the Reiki sessions she falls asleep. On the next day she feels very tired, but she is coming back to receive more Reiki.

This is a natural experience that shows the relaxing effect of Reiki. The tiredness she feels afterward is the result of the transformation taking place within her energy body and its subsequent adjustment.

For instance, when someone goes through surgery because of a serious condition, she does not start her daily activities immediately, nor she can walk or run right away, because her body needs time to recover and adjust to its new state.

The same happens when we work deeply on an energy level: If we are suffering from a disorder, if our own energy is not in a good condition, or if we gathered within so much tiredness over the years, because our energy is being restored in a relatively short period of time, our whole system needs time to adapt to its new and improved condition, so it is normal that for some time we feel tired.

REIKI

AND MEDITATION

Reiki and Meditation

Meditation is a focused state of mind. Here, flexibility is essential and for this reason neither the body nor the focus of our attention is uptight. In an open and soothed posture, our spine elongated, as we focus our mind for the time needed, two things happen:

- The frenetic activity of our thoughts tends to calm down.

- Within the silence we are able to create, we can *see* what else we hold within ourselves.

Our attention is usually focused on our own mental activity. Our daily sleep time is not able to provide the mind with the rest it needs. The rest needed for our mental processes to be at an optimum level comes from the silence we are able to create within our mind, and silence is created in meditation.

Our regular mental activity is conditioned by the constant flow of information coming in from the outside. If we do not set up filters in order to choose what we want to assimilate, and if we do not give the mind the rest it needs for optimal functioning, the cluster of information may drench and distort our perception of the world, ourselves, and our life.

An excess of information conditions our thought, and our thought is a vibration which is constantly affecting our body and determines the kind of experiences we attract to our life.

Within our energy body, the energy wheels known as *chakras* propel our own vital energy as the heart pumps blood throughout our physical body. Each chakra holds certain traits in regard to our instincts, tendencies, and emotions. These energy wheels also contain within themselves certain nucleus that when touched or activated thanks to techniques such as Reiki, yoga, meditation, and others, may unfold fountains of infinite love, extraordinary peace, or outstanding strength. In order to access them, a steady attention and quietude of mind are required. We develop these skills through meditation.

Aware of this, we become independent and our life is deeply transformed. As we practice meditation on a regular basis and our mind calms down, a transformation within our energy takes place, so that peaceful and balanced inner states prevail. On an energy level, these states come closer to the vibrational quality of Reiki, so the Reiki transmission is enhanced.

Why do the Reiki advanced level courses include meditation?

We said that Reiki is distinctive because it flows very well throughout ordered systems, and meditation places order on absolutely everything regarding a human being.

On the other hand, Reiki induces meditative states within the practitioner and the receiver, because it calms the mind.

Meditation is vast and profound, but it basically consists of our attention being taken away from the constant mental activity and steadily directed toward other areas of our system. This process allows us to see what else we hold within ourselves: an extraordinary world to be explored.

As we take our attention away from thoughts, their tendency is to calm down. Therefore, all the feelings associated to thoughts get settled too.

We know that our mind does not rest during the waking state. When we realize that our sleep time also fails to provide the rest needed by the mind, since it is the mind that unfolds the dreaming realm, we can understand the deep rest our mind gets from just a few minutes of meditation.

The vibration of Reiki is pure love. As practitioners, we act as a channel for this energy, and we make its way easier as we meditate and gradually relax any excess of mental and emotional activity. Over time, with meditation, our overall vibration comes closer to the Reiki vibration and we allow a greater flow to be transmitted as we perform a treatment because it finds fewer obstacles on its way through us.

Can I meditate as I perform a Reiki treatment?

Of course you can. You do not need to close your eyes in order to meditate. Every time our attention is highly focused upon any activity we are performing, we are in a meditative state. In fact, this is what we should look for when we perform a Reiki treatment; we should also hold a relaxed physical, mental, and emotional attitude.

Detachment from results is essential. We can keep our spine elongated while being totally focused and aware of whatever is happening, paying attention to the receiver and to our energy sensations.

We already know the technique as we are following all the necessary steps, but we do not need to "think" of whatever is taking place or whatever we expect from the treatment. In this way we will reach deep silence within, and this will allow for a huge Reiki flow.

There is a lot taking place on the seeming silence and quietude of a Reiki session, so many perceptions and sensations that we can become aware of if we are able to create enough inner and outer silence.

Can I continue my Reiki practice without meditating?

Yes, of course. In Reiki nothing really is requested from you. Reiki is just the activation of a skill. The steps we recommend are meant to allow for a greater Reiki flow.

Meditation is not essential for Reiki, but it will improve your Reiki practice and results.

I read this is a "spiritual path." Is that true?

The words "spiritual path" can bring up a whole range of ideas in the mind, and those words probably mean something different for each of us.

A regular Reiki practice helps you dissolve limiting concepts hiding within and allows you to see what else you are, apart from your physical body. As limitations dissolve, your experience is one of greater freedom and you are able to get to deeper states of inner love.

If the person reading this understands that a "spiritual path" is any way of living that allows her to get rid of her limitations, then we can affirm that Reiki may be so. But we need to make it clear that there is no dogma to Reiki and therefore it is not a religion. We do not even need to "believe" in Reiki, since it is a technique that works, regardless of our faith in it.

How can I "empty my mind of thoughts"?

You can give your mind an object to focus on—an image, a sound, a mantra—that allows it to stay alert while remaining focused enough for the mental activity to slow down.

Our attention can be pictured as a floodlight shedding light on whatever we choose. It is usually focused on our thoughts. We can direct the attention wherever we choose, either toward the objects of the world or toward energy centers within the body, in much the same way we handle a video camera.

In meditation we release the attention from the mental turmoil and direct it toward the center of our own chest, toward the movement of our breath, or toward the space between the eyebrows. Or we can give our attention an image, a sound, or a mantra to focus on. When the mental activity begins to slow down it is possible to become aware of our own inner peace, which is always present.

> ***I find no difference between the quietude that takes over when I do Reiki and the stillness I get into when I meditate.***

This is another example of the ideal approach to the Reiki treatments. This person practices meditation and she can feel that the inner states she taps into as she meditates are similar to the inner states that Reiki brings forth as she focuses her attention on the present moment, in silence and free from thoughts.

ATTUNEMENT

EXPERIENCES

Attunement Experiences

A very deep meditative environment is created during the attunement section of the courses. The intense Reiki transmission opens up many energy centers within each person taking the course.

It is possible to enjoy new sensations of the energy running throughout our body, to glimpse lights, to tap into deep meditative states, to feel great heat or a kind of an electrical density due to the powerful Reiki transmission. Sometimes we lose track of time and people who have never done so are able to meditate quietly during the attunement for more than one hour. This is because we were able to bring great stillness to the mind.

Probably the most remarkable experience of an attunement comes from discovering the deep dimension that a human being can reach for. Understanding that we are more than a physical body made of flesh and blood opens up a whole new perspective in life. Moving beyond the physical realm and transcending the personality barrier to discover our own unending resources for strength, security, love, and stillness—regardless of external circumstances—can transform the way we see ourselves and consider our life.

People are often amazed to discover that after an attunement they are able to convey such intense vital energy through the hands and that they can also benefit from it to gradually recover peace and balance.

When I have any subtle perception because of Reiki how do I know it is not auto-suggestion?

Of course auto-suggestion can be of help to relax or get well. Auto-suggestion is defined as "the calling up in the mind of one idea by another, by virtue of some association or of some natural connection between the ideas" and, therefore, we cannot do that regarding something we are actually experiencing for the first time, something that we did not previously know.

The first time we are attuned or the first time we receive a Reiki treatment it can be difficult to describe the sensations that we noticed because they are so new to us—we know that auto-suggestion is not responsible for these new sensations because we have no previous "association or natural connection" to explain them.

When the energy sensations during the attunement or the treatment are subtle, the mind does not consider them as something it already knows, so it may come up with an excuse or it may forget them altogether, because it is not able to define or register them.

Simply observing whatever is happening without judging it is the best attitude. And it is good to write down on a Reiki journal what we felt. With practice and in time, we may come to understand its significance or just remember the nice new sensation we enjoyed.

During the attunement section of the course I lost track of time and of my own body. I felt as if I were floating. What is the reason for this?

Usually our attention is focused on the physical body and the world, but during the attunement you became more aware of your energy body for some time. Both "bodies" fit within each other and constantly affect each other.

As you calm down the mind, it is normal that you may perceive your energy body, which is made out of light. It goes beyond your skin and as your attention dwells in it, you can feel as if you were a formless and extremely light mass that pulsates, that vibrates. It is possible to even notice that you are sloping to a certain direction, while the teacher sees you totally straight: the energy body slightly shifted and because you were more aware of it, you believed you were inclined when it was not like that from the "physical" standpoint.

This is not a matter for concern; it happens due to an adjustment within our system and we always come back to place since both "bodies" are always united until we leave the physical body on the last exhalation. Reiki will never trigger sensations that one is not able to assimilate, since we are working with a very intelligent energy that acts upon a person in a way she can receive it and integrate it.

***During the attunement section I felt my hands
extremely hot and a strong pressure in the space between
my eyebrows.***

The attunement is a very potent Reiki transmission that opens up a series of channels within your energy body. Reiki in such amounts further impels the energy wheels or chakras. You will feel the heat within your hands because the chakras within your palms have been opened and activated and they are allowing Reiki to flow through them. You might feel pressure in the space between your eyebrows when the ajna chakra right at that spot is opening up on a deeper level. When these centers open in the body, there is a definite physical sensation.

At the space between the eyebrows we can notice a concentrated density or a keen pressure that might last minutes, hours, or even days. This is a very positive sign that the qualities held deep within this chakra are starting to unfold for the sake of your inner growth.

Here we are talking about the unfoldment of knowledge, and not intellectual knowledge acquired through books, but your own inner knowledge that allows a deep understanding of the circumstances in which you live. This knowledge leads you to answers to your questions such as Who am I? Why am I here?

I noticed as if inside the crown of my head I was being raked, but I know you did not touch me.

The chakra at the crown of the head is another important center that is activated as a result of the Reiki attunement. The sensation this person is trying to describe took place several times at this particular course and it indicates that a certain aspect of this crown chakra is opening. This is a very physical sensation, although it is not painful at all. It is a powerful energy movement.

I felt "anguish" within my chest and my breath moved in and out in an unusual way; my body would hold the breath in for some time.

The sensation she describes is not actual anguish but just another opening movement of the heart chakra, located in the center of our chest. As it opens up, we may notice a heartwarming explosion of energy.

In life, we "protect" our heart by building a shell around it. As the shell "breaks apart" to allow the opening of the chakra, we may feel as if something is cracking up. There is great love within that place and it can unfold and intoxicate us with its beauty if we allow for this process.

The spontaneous movements of the breath are known as pranayama. We can stop these kind of adjustments if they feel uncomfortable, although it is good that we let them take place because our body knows what kind of opening movements restitute our optimum energy flow. Our body lets these movements be as soon as we allow for the silence it needs. The spontaneous, highly beneficial breath affects the mind and triggers cleansing processes within us.

> ***Following the attunement at the first-level course I found myself in love with everyone and everything.***

This awakening of love is a common experience following a Reiki course. In the course, we dive deep into this energy and many energy centers containing previously trapped fountains of love are opened. Together with the mental stillness we tapped into, we can enjoy something that the Sufis affirm is within everyone and everything; they explain that everything is born from love and with the right vision anyone can perceive it.

We can enjoy this experience within the intimacy of our own heart and, understanding what is happening to us, there is no need to hug everyone, exclaiming "I love you!" These awakening sensations are highly purifying to our physical body and they are so rewarding that it is not possible to forget them.

> ***It was a very interesting process. I felt warmth and energy moving around.***

During the attunement section, the energy sensations usually are not subtle at all. They are very clear, almost physical and palpable. It is always amazing to discover them and it is actually easy to perceive the energy movements when we create inner silence, and especially when we transmit Reiki.

I am impressed at what I felt. I had never been in touch with these things and I was not expecting any great experience from the course.

This is again a normal reaction following the attunement. All the sensations that we perceive during a course are a remembrance of something we had forgotten.

During childhood we would have more easily perceived luminous colors or felt the movement of energy. As we grow up, we learn to direct our focus mainly to the physical reality, which usually limits our awareness and our access to the multiple possibilities that the "energy world" offers.

For this reason, the Reiki attunement is a reawakening to ourselves and to our skills; this is why taking a Reiki course and developing the method is so satisfying and life transforming.

I felt warmth within my chest, pressure and warmth within my head and hands. With my eyes closed I had insights of colorful lights as well as of a bright white light.

The heat and pressure are the result of the intense energy movement that is taking place within you. Again, with your eyes closed you are having insights of colorful lights because you perceive your energy body, which is luminous; the bright white light may be the light of Reiki coming through you.

I saw an eye in the space between my eyebrows and I felt a stream of light coming through. I felt warmth and a lot of peace and stillness.

The chakra at the space between the eyebrows is usually referred to as the "third eye." When you are able to perceive light that does not belong to the spectrum of visible energies, you do not see it with your physical eyes but you are using a faculty of this one chakra. This is why we are able to "see" bright sharp images within ourselves, with our eyes closed, when we tap into deep meditative states. Some people are able to see through this chakra even while their physical eyes are open.

The heat, the peace, and the stillness are because of the flow of Reiki energy.

It was fascinating to me that I was able to think about nothing. My mind went blank.

This is a sign that you entered a deep meditative state, where your attention shifted from the constant mental activity to another space within yourself. At such states, you are keenly aware of yourself and of your own presence, unaware of the labels that usually define you and limit you to a great degree. Such mental stillness provides your body with an extraordinary rest and a palpable peace. It is wonderful to find out that we can still "function" in this world without so many thoughts!

I felt as if I were swaying, but the truth is that I was not moving at all. I felt a lot of heat and some dizziness. Sometimes I felt as if I were floating around.

That is not a physical movement, but your energy body slightly shifting, searching for an adjustment. That is the reason for your "dizziness," but if you pay attention to it you will notice that it is not like a regular dizziness but just another sensation of your energy body.

Also, the feeling of "floating around" is because you become more aware of your energy body than of the physical body. As we already mentioned, the energy body is light and it goes beyond our skin; since it does not have physical weight, we feel as if we were suspended in the air.

As I was being attuned, I saw that a golden light was being poured within my head. As it reached the center of my forehead, it whirled inside a wheel of light for a few seconds.

This is exactly what takes place at every attunement: A great stream of Reiki is transmitted; it enters the crown of the head. On its way, it reinforces the chakras, it fills up any existing energy vacuum and it unlocks any energy blockages. This person felt how the chakra within the space between her eyebrows was intensely activated due to the massive Reiki flow. As the chakras whirl, they impel the energy on a spiral movement through the energy channels.

> *I felt great inner peace and rest. I could listen to my own silence and I had no notion of my physical boundaries.*

Once again, the inner peace and rest are the first consequence after calming down your thoughts. It is beautiful the way you describe how you can listen to your own inner silence, so restorative. Any notions of physical reality are lost and that is why you perceive no limits. Actually, in such deep states we are able to release limiting thought and behavior patterns.

> *For me this has been impressive; a very positive experience and learning that may help me and others when I do Reiki on them. Perceiving the light and the energy running throughout my body is something extremely enjoyable. This left me experiencing a relaxed and meditative physical and mental state.*

Feeling the energy may be a very physical and clear perception. On some occasions, its work is very subtle and we may think that we do not even feel it. At other times, we are amazed at how palpable it is.

We said that the vibrational frequency of Reiki is very close to the vibration of love. That is why as it fills us up, we feel peace, relief, relaxation, and contentment. Reiki brings about meditative states, and for this reason our mind relaxes and both the Reiki practitioner and the receiver rest deeply.

> *I saw a conduit made of white light extend across myself and it powerfully pierced my hands and feet.*

Here, this person was able to see, as Reiki was being transmitted, that the light was making its way through her own hands and feet. As we see, it also goes through the soles of the feet; it actually fills the whole body up, but it draws in such a way that it guarantees a greater flow through the palms of the hands.

> *I was thrilled and I almost cried. I felt a lot of warmth, energy, and light being poured on me, although my eyes were closed; extremely pleasing sensations that I never had before.*

> *I also discovered my other body, the "nonphysical" one. It was very exciting.*

Again, this appreciation comes because we are recognizing aspects of our own deepest nature. The heat, the energy, and the light that she is able to perceive with her eyes closed are related to her energy body, made out of light, as well as to the Reiki light filling up her whole system.

Marta Martín was born in Valladolid (Spain) and she lived in New York for seven years. Professionally she worked as the Editorial Manager and Chief Translator of a course on meditation and self-development. She studied Eastern philosophies and meditation, as well as various holistic therapies such as Resonance Repatterning or both the Tibetan and Japanese Reiki styles.

She recently translated and published "Un Jardín Más Allá del Paraíso – Poemas de Amor de Rumi", the Spanish version of "A Garden Beyond Paradise — Love poems of Rumi" by Jonathan Star. She taught Reiki Courses in New York and she is currently teaching them in Spain, where she also offers series of workshops on "The Secret of Thought: How to Use Your Mind to Improve Your Life."